ENGLAND
of One Hundred Years Ago
PHOTOGRAPH
COLLECTION

C000216774

SWINDON

SELECTED BY DAVID BUXTON

ALAN SUTTON

First published in the United Kingdom in 1992
by Alan Sutton Publishing Limited
Phoenix Mill, Stroud, Gloucestershire

First published in the United States of America
by Alan Sutton Publishing Incorporated
83 Washington Avenue, Dover, New Hampshire

Copyright © Alan Sutton Publishing Limited, 1992

British Library and Library of Congress
Cataloguing in Publication Data applied for

ISBN 0-7509-03082

Typesetting and origination by
Alan Sutton Publishing Limited
Graphics and Design Department.
Printed in Great Britain by
Bath Colour Books.

Some blemishes have been removed by extreme enlargement of the image to individual pixel
level, with careful computer graphics surgery to mend scratches, foxing, or other damage to the
photographic image.

ENGLAND
of One Hundred Years Ago
VOLUME EIGHT

Swindon

The photograph collection of England of One Hundred Years Ago is an attempt to find and produce some of the best images in existence from late Victorian times up to the onset of the First World War. The country has been split into the traditional counties and this volume, numbered 8, represents Swindon.

The criteria for selection are quality and clarity in the image together with subject interest. An attempt has been made to ensure a reasonable geographical balance within the area covered, but it has to be admitted that some areas were much more photographed than others.

The printed images are intended to be used for framing, although some people may wish to buy additional separate prints for framing by using the order form at the back of the book, and to keep this book intact. If the order form becomes separated from the book please write to the Phoenix Mill address advising the volume number and plate number you require.

The reproductions in this book are obtained by digital scanning and computer enhancement. Some blemishes have been removed by extreme enlargement of the image to individual pixel level, with careful computer graphics surgery to mend scratches, foxing, or other damage to the photographic image. The pictures on the facing page show a scratch, enlarged and repaired. Some damage, or blemishes in an otherwise interesting photograph are beyond reasonable repair, and have been left.

The monochrome image is then further enhanced by being artificially separated and printed in a four colour process with a sepia bias. The result is a high quality image with visual depth. The finished printed image is then protected by a careful application of matt varnish to reduce fading and to add protection. The paper is a super-calendared, acid free, matt art of 170 grammes weight per square metre.

The contents of the photographs remain totally genuine and the enhancement and surgery are used only to mend damage and not to create artificial images!

Swindon at the turn of the century was the largest town in Wiltshire and one of the most important, industrially, in southern and central England. Its rapid rise to prominence followed the arrival of the railway and the siting of the Great Western Railway works in the town in the 1840s. These photographs show busy Victorian and Edwardian streets, the town's large shops and the terraced houses of the factory workers, the trams and the railway workshops. All around Swindon was the rural expanse of North Wiltshire, an area of small villages and farms, largely unchanged for centuries. This contrasting rural area is the subject of another volume in this series.

Contents

Acknowledgements.
We would like to thank the following who have kindly allowed us to reproduce their photographs in this publication: Geoff Parker, Peter Sheldon, Wiltshire Library and Museum Service.

Plate 1. REGENT STREET
Swindon, *c.* 1905

Plate 2. 'LORD OF THE ISLES'
A famous broad gauge locomotive built at Swindon
in 1851 and seen here in the 1870's

030294
16:20
N0 00.34

·3.99 1
·3.99 ST
·20.00 M
·16.01 CG

Plate 3. TRAM STOP
Regent Circus, *c*. 1905

Plate 4. WALKING HOME
Commercial Road, *c.* 1913

Plate 5. GRAND OPENING SALE!
Keogh Brothers' shop at 45 Bridge Street, 1901

Plate 6. CROWDED STREET
Busy scene in Cromwell Street, *c*. 1913

Plate 7. SWINDON RAMBLERS
Swindon Cycle Club, 1891

Plate 8. A QUIET LANE
Drove Road, *c.* 1910

Plate 9. HURRY ABOARD PLEASE!
Tram in Park Lane, *c.* 1905

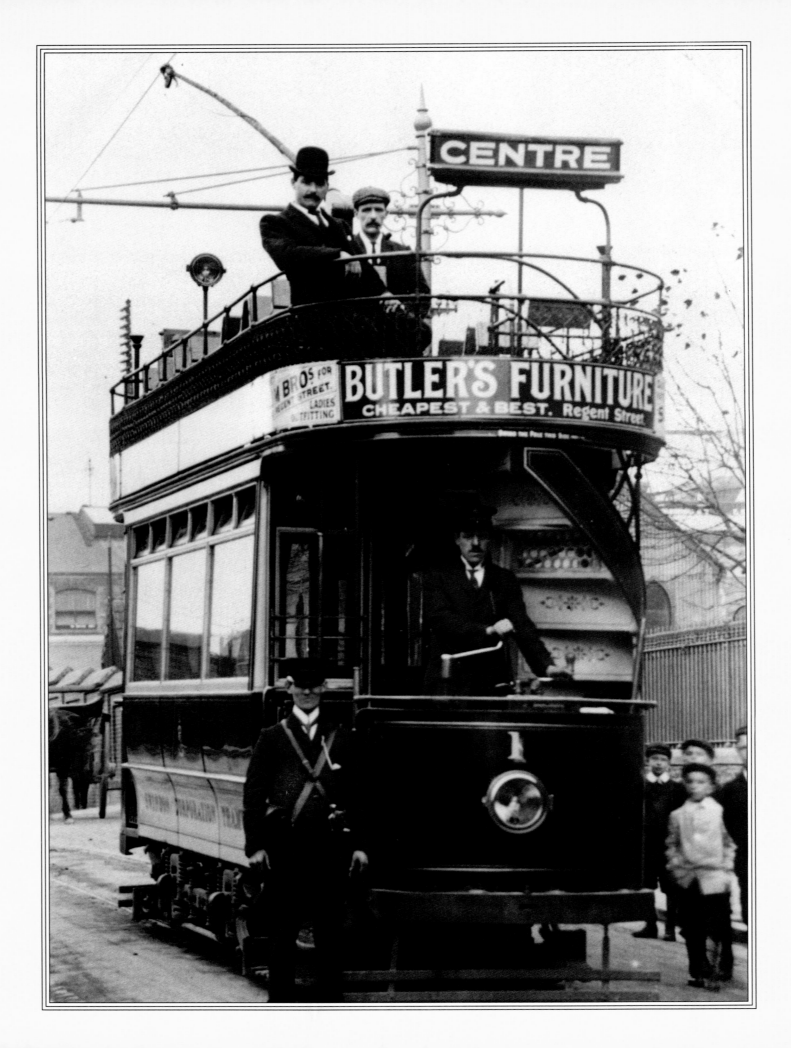

Plate 10. BOATING IN THE PARK
Coate Reservoir, *c.* 1900

Plate 11. THE BOTTLING ROOM
Brown and Plummer's, Old Town, *c.* 1919

Plate 12. PRIZE WINNING DISPLAY
F. Sparkes, Regent Street, winners of a window-dressing competition in
1910

Plate 13. CHILDREN ON THE BRIDGE
The old Golden Lion Bridge, 1905

Plate 14. END OF THE SHIFT
Workers leaving the railway works through Emlyn Square, *c.* 1905

Plate 15. SWINDON STEAM
Goods engine built in Swindon in 1873, seen here in 1902

Plate 16. THE PAINT SHOP
Locomotives awaiting a final coat of paint in the GWR workshops,
c. 1895

Plate 17. TRIP DAY
Railway workers and their families waiting for the train to take them to
the sea-side on the works' holiday, *c.* 1912

Plate 18. MEETING FATHER OUT OF WORK
Workers leaving the GWR factories, *c.* 1913

Plate 19. CARPENTERS' SHOP
Everything needed by the GWR in wood was made in this workshop,
c. 1895

Plate 20. THE OUTING
Railwaymens' families by the Mechanic's Institute, boarding buses for a
trip, *c.* 1912

Plate 21. HIGH STREET TRAM
High Street, *c.* 1912

Plate 22. THE IRONMONGER'S SHOP
J. Lott and Sons, 50 Regent Street, *c.* 1910

Plate 23. THE SWINDON MAIL
Postman leaving the Head Post Office to deliver the morning's mail,
c. 1905

Plate 24. STANDING IN THE ROAD
Fleet Street, *c.* 1913

Plate 25. HIGH CLASS GROCER
H. Freeth and Son, Fleet Street, *c.* 1903

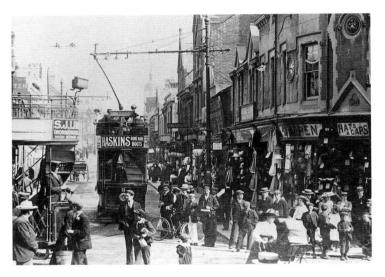

Plate 26. TRAM CENTRE
Opening of the Swindon Tram Centre, 1904

Plate 27. LOITERING
Regent Street, *c.* 1905

Plate 28. STREET CORNER KIDS
Curtis Street, *c.* 1913